W9-BTB-726

Golf in the Year
2000

With the compliments of

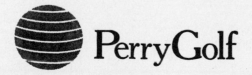

the provider of

Luxury Golf Travel for the next Millennium

Golf in the Year

2000

or, What We Are Coming To

By J. McCullough (J.A.C.K.)

"Two paths hath life, and well the theme
May mournful thoughts inspire;
For ah, the past is but a dream,
The future a desire."

From the Arabic.

Rutledge Hill Press®

Nashville, Tennessee

Copyright © 1998 by Rutledge Hill Press®

This book is a reprint of the book *Golf in the Year 2000*, originally published in 1892 by T. Fisher Unwin in London, England. The cover design, page design, and inside artwork were specially commissioned for this edition by Rutledge Hill Press® and are the copyrighted property of Rutledge Hill Press®.

Published in Nashville, Tennessee, by Rutledge Hill Press®, 211 Seventh Avenue North, Nashville, Tennessee 37219.

Distributed in Canada by H. B. Fenn & Company, Ltd., 34 Nixon Road, Bolton, Ontario L7E 1W2.

Distributed in Australia by The Five Mile Press Pty., Ltd., 22 Summit Road, Noble Park, Victoria 3174.

Distributed in New Zealand by Tandem Press, 2 Rugby Road, Birkenhead, Auckland 10.

Distributed in the United Kingdom by Verulam Publishing, Ltd., 152a Park Street Lane, Park Street, St. Albans, Hertfordshire AL2 2AU.

Typography by Compass Communications, Inc.
Illustrations by David Wariner

Library of Congress Cataloging-in-Publication Data

McCullough, J.
    Golf in the year 2000, or, What we are coming to / by J. McCullough (J.A.C.K.).
        p.   cm.
    ISBN 1-55853-664-7 (hardcover)
    I. Title.
    PR4964.M87G65   1998
    823'.8—dc21   98-25220
                                                              CIP

Printed in the United States of America
2 3 4 5 6 7 8 9—02 01 00 99 98

Editor's Foreword

Most of the many golf books coming out in the 1990s bear an uncanny resemblance to one another. They include "revolutionary" instructional books; compendiums of clichéd quotes, well-worn anecdotes, or previously published articles; and coffee-table works celebrating great golfers, major tournaments, and prestigious courses. As versatile and diverse as these books are, they lack a sense of originality. Of course, an occasional work of contemporary fiction or journalistic investigation offers some element of intrigue, but there is much fertile ground waiting to be explored—so much left for one's imagination.

One search for imaginative literature takes us back more than one hundred years to this book, *Golf in the Year 2000*, a work of vivid fantasy that was originally published in London in 1892. It has the feel of a Jules Verne or H. G. Wells novel. Although it can be read quickly because of its brevity and lighthearted tone, to do so is to miss the revelatory nature of the text. These insights give *Golf in the Year 2000* a legitimate claim·as the perfect "new" book for the twenty-first century. This is a book whose time has come again.

I came across this book serendipitously, which naturally added a touch of fascination. At the 1997 Golf Collector's Society Convention in Nashville, several exhibiting dealers were showcasing shelves of decades-old books, many of them now out of print and a few falling apart at the seams. Running my fingers along the spines of the books on display, I paused and pulled out a fairly recent facsimile of this book, presuming it to be another attempt to capitalize on the current wave of millennium madness. After about five minutes of delightful reading, I turned to the title page and saw that the book had originally been published in the nineteenth century.

Golf in the Year 2000 is the tale of one Alexander J. Gibson, an avid nineteenth-century Scottish golfer who falls into a deep sleep, Rip Van Winkle-like, in 1892. He reawakens in the twenty-first century (or on the threshold of the twenty-first century for those who believe the new century actually begins with the year 2001) where golf is still cherished but the world has undergone a number of societal and technological changes eerily consistent with present-day reality. Giving away any more of the plot would spoil the fun of reading this book, so prepare to be enlightened and entertained at your own pace. Savor the experience of a golf book that truly is unique.

—Mike Towle, editor (1998)

PREFACE

Why this book was written, I don't know. It's not meant to instruct; you'll have no doubt of that, after you have read it. It's not meant to—I don't even know what it's not meant to do, any more than what it is. It's not even to "supply a long felt want"—that's the correct phrase, I think. Read it, and see what you think it's meant to do, because I don't.

I began with the intention of having a moral, but I hadn't gone very far when I forgot what the moral was, so I left it out. Of course that's not to say that the book is immoral—far from it.

When I showed the MS. to a friend, he asked

me, "What will a man do, then, who doesn't like golf?" He thought he had me, but he hadn't. I answered him in the Scotch fashion by "asking him another." "Had he ever heard of a man who, once having played golf, did not like it?" Ah! had him there! He had to admit he had not, so that settled it. I'm afraid this is rather a poor preface, dear reader, but you see I'm not very accustomed to writing prefaces; but there's one good point about it, though I says it as shouldn't, it's short.

J.A.C.K. (1892)

Contents

Golf in the Year
2000

CHAPTER I.

IN 1892.

Well, my game was not so very bad after all. It was that fellow Brown's infernal luck. The way he holed long putts would have put a saint off his game. So ran my thoughts after dinner. When I first came in I had sworn that I had never played a worse game — vowed that I couldn't hit a ball, and that I'd have a bonfire of my clubs in the back green, or give them away without a pound of tea. I was sick of the sight of them.

Brown himself came in by and by, however, and

after sundry whiskies, hot, I began to think I had been playing quite a good game after all—indeed, I finished up by challenging him to play me once more on the morrow. Ah! that to-morrow! How many matches have been fixed for it that are still things of the future! How "many a slip" there is! In my own case, for instance——But I must not anticipate, *à nos moutons*, as they say in the land of "the darned Mounseer." When Brown left I had another pipe (and—shall I say?—another half-one) before turning in.

Next—but I think what happened next morning requires a new chapter.

CHAPTER II.

When I awoke next morning I felt a curious sensation, viz., "pins and needles" all over my body, like
those in your foot when it goes to sleep. I felt very
stiff, too — in fact, I could not move, and lay wondering what the matter was.

The room I was in also seemed strange to me.
The first thing I noticed was the roof, which was for
all the world like a large white saucer reversed. The
room, I may mention, was in semi-darkness, as it

was only lighted by a small square window above the door.

Gradually the pricking sensation began to get less, until I could move my limbs a little. And now, behold—here I was "in a box" and no mistake, for I found myself to be lying in what I took to be a sort of coffin. I began to wonder if this was not a dream, and tried to recall what I had been doing the night before. I remembered Brown coming in and talking over our match, and I distinctly remembered going to bed. "Well," I thought, "I suppose it's some joke of Brown's; but whether it's time to laugh or not, I don't know."

My next discovery—rather a startling one for a man that had gone to bed a few hours before clean-shaven—was that I had a beard. And such a beard! Why, it would have stuffed a dining-room suite with half-a-dozen sofas in it. My hair, too, as you shall presently learn, looked as if it had not been cut for a century. And has the reader ever reflected what that description would imply, if taken literally? Perhaps he has not had the chance to picture it to himself,

*My next discovery—rather a startling one for a man that had gone
to bed a few hours before clean-shaven—was that I had a beard.
And such a beard!*

whereas I—but never mind. All I need say is that I lay
for several minutes lost in astonishment at the growth
of my beard.

But I soon began to think I had better get up;
and the next difficulty was, how to get out of my box.
All my limbs were very stiff, and, moreover, the lid of
the box—or coffin, whichever it was—came up as far
as my armpits, leaving my face alone exposed. All I
could do was to try and work my way out by this open
part, which I found no easy task. At last, however, I
was out. Sitting down on the top of my former
prison, I gave my legs a stretch. I *did* feel cramped
and sore.

Still wondering as to my whereabouts, I
presently thought I would have a look round, and see
what kind of place I was in. I got up and moved
towards the door, which, when I had come within a
foot or so, suddenly and without any warning shot
back into the wall. Thus I found myself at once in a
large, handsomely-furnished room. "Well!" I thought
to myself, "whoever has planned this joke has done
the thing well, that's one comfort!"

Looking round, I saw a huge glass globe half full of water, which bulged out from one wall of the room, with a raised daïs of white marble round the outside. It was quite shut in, except for an opening at the side presumably for getting out and entering at. This suggested the matutinal tub. In I got accordingly, and on my grasping a steel rod which stretched across it, the opening closed, and the whole structure began to fly round about and backwards and forwards, till I was almost drowned. After going for about a minute—it seemed hours to me—the churning process stopped, and the window, if I may call it so, opened. You may be sure I was not long in getting out, bruised, battered, and half-drowned. On recovering myself I proceeded to look about for some more seemly clothing than the night-shirt in which—the place being altogether strange to me, and my own habiliments invisible—I had been wandering about until I entered the bath. A wardrobe which stood in one corner would not be persuaded to open; but, to add to my astonishment, I presently found what I wanted on a chair. I picked up first a shirt, which seemed to be made of a sort of silk, very finely woven. This I put on, and next donned a pair of black knee-breeches—which seemed to be made of the same material as the shirt, but of stronger texture—and black stockings, also of the same stuff. Thus attired, I approached a toilet table on which was a large looking-glass, &c. At first sight of my head of hair and beard I went into roars of laughter. For, I am sure, ten minutes, I simply stood and held my sides and shouted.

Hearing an exclamation, I turned round and saw standing in an open doorway—not the one I had myself come in by—the figure of a man, clad like myself as far as the knee-breeches went, and with a loose sort of jacket made of the same stuff, buttoned up to the throat. He was very white, and looked all the more odd because he had not a particle of hair on his face, or his head either, for the matter of that, barring a sort of tonsure of sandy-coloured hair round the skull from one ear to the other.

This apparition stood leaning against the side of the door, and gazing at me for some seconds. He then darted across the room and disappeared—only to reappear, however, in a moment, from the anteroom where I had been lying. The door closed so quickly after him that to my unaccustomed eyes—which have got used to the sight since—he seemed for the moment to have vanished.

He now came slowly forward, and, sitting down on a chair, gazed at me. Never a word did he speak, so I at last broke silence myself.

"Well," I said, "this is a capital joke as far as it has gone, but I would like it explained. Where am I, and what's it all about? I've barked my shins getting out of my bunk" (as, indeed, I had, and no wonder)— "I've been nearly drowned in that patent bath of yours, and, pray, how do you account for this?" I added, tugging my beard and looking fiercely at him.

His lips moved in reply; but what he said sounded more like a soliloquy than an answer.

"At last, at last! Living, moving, speaking! Just as they said he might some day! And yet—a man that has been lying seemingly dead for the last ten years to my knowledge, and goodness only knows for how long before!"

"He must be a maniac!" I thought to myself; "and this will be their toggery, and that bath affair something for cooling their brains."

"Ten years!" I said, aloud; "is that all? Say a century while you're about it! But would you be so good as to tell me what or whose house this is?"

"Certainly. It belongs to your humble servant." And here he handed me a card, on which was written, "W. Adams, C.I.G.C."

"Well, Mr. W. Adams, C.I.G.C., I would like to understand to what happy circumstance I am indebted for becoming your uninvited guest."

"Sir," he said, tremulously, "you found yourself, did you not, lying in a box in that room?" He pointed to the anteroom.

"Yes," I admitted.

"Well, in that room you have, to my certain knowledge, been lying for the last ten years," he went on. "You have been examined periodically by members of the medical faculty, who have always found a certain amount of heat in your body, and your heart beating, though faintly. When I bought this house ten years ago you were lying there, and it was part of the arrangement that I was not to disturb you, and that I must have you examined at the usual intervals."

I sat down and looked at him. It was now my turn to be dumbfounded. When I had to some extent collected my scattered wits, I said:

"Will you kindly inform me what year this is?"

"It is" (and he referred to a pocket almanac as he spoke) "the twenty-fifth of March, 2000."

"What!" I cried, "the year 2000? This is rather too steep! What are you talking about?"

For all answer he jumped up, crying, "The package, the package!" and rushed into the ante-room. Presently he came back, carrying a long-shaped envelope.

"This," he said, "has been lying under your head."

On the cover was written: "Not to be opened until the unhappy Alexander J. Gibson either revives or expires."

It was my mother's handwriting; but ah! how faded the ink!

"We are now at liberty to open it," said my companion. And hastily, with trembling fingers, he did so. Inside was a paper bearing the words:

"This is to certify that Alexander John Gibson fell into a trance on the night of Thursday, the 24th day of March, 1892. We have done all we could to revive him, but without success.

A-------B------

C-------D------

Signed this 3oth day of March, 1892."

When he had finished reading he looked up.

"A hundred and eight years," he said, solemnly. "How unheard-of!"

"Thursday, the twenty-fourth of March!" I said. "I tell you that was yesterday. I distinctly remember all that happened. This must be a dream, or you are deceiving me—you mean to—"

But he interrupted me.

"Your own senses tell you it is no dream," he said, almost sternly. "Nor shall you long want for proof that it is, indeed, the twenty-first century. Come with me."

"In the first place," I said, "I would like this removed," indicating my beard. Can you take me to a barber's?"

"A barber?" he replied. "Ah! to be sure—you lived a century ago. We don't have such things now. This will serve your purpose." Going forward to the table he lifted a small bottle, and, unscrewing the stopper, drew out a sort of flat brush. This he drew gently down one side of my face, and thereupon motioned me to look in the glass. The sight that met my gaze was even more ludicrous than at first. On the right side of my face not a vestige of a hair was to be seen, while the other was, as I had seen it before, covered with a huge bushy beard.

I asked him what magic this was.

"Only a preparation," he replied, with a smile, "for removing and keeping down the growth of hair. We only require to use it once a week or once a fortnight. I've heard my grandfather talk of the old fashion of shaving, and it always struck me as being very clumsy and a great bother."

"Well," I said, "since you've begun you had

better finish, as I don't want to go about like this."

He laughed, and, applying the brush again, in a second had my face as clean as a baby's.

"You'd better brush your hair now," he said, handing me a pair of brushes.

My hair, I think I said before, was very long, and looked like a huge stable mop. With a touch from these brushes, however, it began to assume more civilised proportions; and when I finished brushing I looked as if I had just had my hair cut.

"Something new, too?" I said, laying down the brushes.

"No, those aren't a very recent invention. They always keep the hair the same length, and you can alter the length to suit yourself by this simple means." Here he showed me a small dial on the backs of the brushes with figures on it.

"But where does all the hair go to?" I inquired.

"Oh, it is destroyed; the same liquid that is in that bottle is in the brushes, and it destroys the hair whenever it comes in contact with it. But put on this jacket," he went on. "It is fortunate we are much of the same build; for the present my wardrobe is at your service."

I put on my jacket, and, looking about me, said:

"I don't see any boots or shoes; would you be good enough—"

"Ah! how stupid of me!" he replied, going to the wardrobe which I had been unable to open. On his touching it twice, the door slid back, and he produced a pair of shoes, the uppers of which seemed to be made of the same stuff as the rest of the clothing, while the soles were of a hard sort of gutta-percha. I put them on, and found they fitted perfectly.

"Now," he said, "if you are ready we will go down and have some food, as I expect you'll be hungry. You deserve to be, at any rate." And I agreed with him there. "It's just about my regular meal-time anyway," he added, looking at a signet ring on his left hand; "6.34. The days are stretching out."

"May I look at that?" I said, for I saw that he had told the hour by the ring.

"Certainly," he replied; "had you not even watches in your days?"

"Oh, yes, we had, but this is very neat."

It was an ordinary sized signet ring with the figures 6.34 on it. As I looked it changed to 6.35, and those were the only figures to be seen. How they managed to get all the works into such small compass I don't know. I returned it to him, and he slipped it on to his finger.

"It's just about my regular meal-time anyway," he added, looking at
a signet ring on his left hand; "6:34. The days are stretching out."

CHAPTER III.

He motioned with his hand for me to precede him. I moved towards the door, which as usual opened at my approach, and we stood in a large well-appointed hall. It was very high, and seemed to be lighted in some way from the roof, which was a large white dome, planned in the same style as the other two rooms, but on a larger scale. The light—it was a bright electric white—seemed to be shed from all parts equally.

35

"Ah! you admire our light," said my companion, seeing my look of wonder. "That is a capital contrivance. It is electric light behind that glass dome, and we have a wonderful little machine, so placed as to catch only daylight, which under the action of light, keeps up a quick rotation. It is connected with an electric current, and as the rotation gets slower, which it does naturally as the light fades, the current is gradually turned on. The slower it gets, the stronger the current and consequently the light. When it ceases altogether the artificial light is at its strongest, and is equal to daylight. So you see we have always the same light—there is no twilight indoors."

I could not quite follow him, but it seemed to me that, when the one light faded, it quietly turned on the other light to take its place, which it really did. A very convenient arrangement, I thought. They are a wonderful people nowadays.

As we were still standing a gong sounded; it seemed to play a tune—what it was, I don't know. I'm not at all musical—at least I wasn't a century ago. Like old Dr. Todhunter, I only knew two tunes.

Eh; what were they, did you say? One was "God Save
the Queen," and the other wasn't, and I only knew
it was "God Save the Queen" because I saw the people stand up. It's a very funny thing, but they seem
to have missed out the musical part of my composi-
tion: where my bump for music should have been,
there's a decided hollow instead. I remember once
staying at a fashionable watering-place—if there is
one thing I hate it's fashionable watering-places—
and that fashionable watering-place had a band.
How I did hate that band! As soon as I got up it
began to play, and it didn't stop till I went to bed,
and always the same tune, of course; "the other
wasn't," except when it played "God Save the
Queen." Oh, yes, I knew it was "God Save the
Queen," because I saw the people stand, and I was
always glad to hear it, as I knew it was the last. I got
almost to know it—at least I thought I did, and one
night I thought I'd show how clever I was, and stood
up when I thought they had begun it; but it wasn't,
so, as I didn't like to sit down again, I took my hat
and went off. But to return.

"Ah! that dinner at last," said Mr. Adams: "follow me."

"But look here," I said, "how about your people?
They'll wonder who the deuce I am!"

"Oh," he said, "don't trouble yourself on that
score. I've only a sister who stays with me, and she
is away just now, so we'll have the whole place to
ourselves."

As he spoke he walked on to a square red rug at
one side of the hall between two pillars. I did like-
wise, and we at once descended to the floor below.

We were now in a hall very similar to the one we
had left. The walls, which were coated with a kind of
enamel, had a dado of black at the foot which gradually shaded off into white towards the top. We crossed
the hall and went into a large dining-room, where
there was a table laid out. Mr. Adams motioned me to
a seat, which I took, nothing loath, as I began to feel
not a little hungry. The walls of this room were the
same as the hall, only the colour was a dark bronze,
getting lighter near the roof or dome. It was furnished
with large heavy furniture, with an eye to comfort

evidently, judging from the couches, settees, &c., with which the room abounded. There were also three large mirrors reaching from floor to ceiling on each of the three walls. The fourth was taken up by the window, which was almost the breadth of the room.

The table, which was round, was set for two, and there was a large fern in the centre, round which were some vases with white flowers that gave out a most delicious perfume. It all looked familiar enough, but after taking our seats my companion pressed a finger on the table, and immediately a gap yawned in front of us. The table seemed to be made of three concentric circular pieces, and the middle one sank down through the floor, leaving intact the outer one, which formed the edge of the complete table, and the "hub," on which the flowers were. The "dumb waiter" portion presently reappeared, bearing two plates of soup on it.

"You see we don't require servants to wait on us nowadays," said Mr. Adams. "Two men manage the whole of my household. There are so many machines to minimise labour, that they have quite taken the place of servants, and our food, you know, is all sent in ready cooked."

After we had finished our soup he pushed his plate in front of him, and I did the same. He again pressed the table with his finger; the plates disappeared, and up came the second course. So it went on through an excellent dinner, which I did full justice to. I must not forget to mention the drink. By our sides were placed two small syphons. When I first saw them I breathed a fervent prayer inwardly that it might not turn out that the people among whom I had come to life again were wholly given over to teetotalism. My fears were quickly allayed by my host saying:

"Try that champagne and tell me what you think of it."

I did as he bade me, and found it a first-rate brand.

"No new invention about this," I said, smacking my lips.

"No," he replied; "the teetotalers have always been trying to palm off on us some new drink or other, but without success. We always come back to the old tipple."

"You smoke?" queried my host, rising as we had finished dinner. "Very well, then; let us go into the smoking-room."

We went across the hall into another room, smaller than the dining-room, but just as comfortably furnished, in which a cheerful fire burned. It was the first fire I had seen, and I asked him if this was the only one in the house.

"Yes," he replied; "as a matter of fact it is. The rest of the house is heated by pipes and hot air, but I always have an old-fashioned fire in this room from choice. It makes a room so nice and home-like."

We drew our chairs towards the fire, and he, pulling out a cigar case, offered me a cigar. I now felt more at home than I had done since I awoke among so many strange sights and novelties.

"It's very odd," I remarked, after a short silence, "that I am sitting here after lying for more than a century as one dead; and still more so that I distinctly remember all that happened on the last day of my former existence, as if it were indeed yesterday. Brown and his long putts, too. Oh, I simply threw away that match." I was talking rather to myself than to my companion in thus musing on the past; but the effect on him was magical.

"Long putts!" he repeated after me in amaze. Then, starting forward in his chair, "Are you a golfer?" he asked, earnestly.

"Yes," I replied, "I used to play a sort of decent game at times."

"By Jove! Let me shake hands with you." And he wrung my hand effusively. "A nineteenth-century golfer in this age! Ah! what luck has been yours! I think you'll own it's been worth living for when I take you round a bit. We'll have a few new things in the golfing line to show you, or I'm much mistaken."

"Indeed," I said, "in my day they thought they had got golf almost to perfection. I suppose you still use the bulger?"

"The bulger?" he queried—"I have never heard of it."

"Is it possible you never saw a bulger? I must bring it out. It's a capital invention, though I don't use one myself from principle. The face of the head is convex, and it matters not whether you heel or toe a ball, they always go straight. I reason that if you don't hit a ball fair, you deserve to go off the line and get punished for it; so I've always stuck to the old straight face, and when I do pull a ball off the course, and lose the hole by it, I have the satisfaction of knowing I've acted up to my principles—though I am beginning, I'll allow, to think it's not much satisfaction after all, especially when it comes to handing over your half-crown. I think I'll really have to take to the bulgers in the end."

"Ah," he said, smothering a yawn, as if he wasn't much interested in the bulger, "I expect golf in your days and golf in ours are two very different things. We manage everything so much better nowadays. But you are fortunate in being under my roof, as I am the chief inspector of golf clubs. It is a government appointment, and that's what the C.I.G.C. on my card stands for."

"Indeed!" I said. "Are golf clubs under government?"

"Yes," he answered, "I have about a hundred inspectors under me, and every club has to be examined and reported on once every three months. It is no easy matter, considering that almost every town in Great Britain has a golfing green. But to-morrow we will have a round on whichever course you wish. What ones used you to play on?"

"I know almost all the Scotch greens," I answered, "and a few of the English."

"Ah, then, I will show you something to-morrow," he said, rising; "and in the meantime, if you have finished your smoke, I will take you to a room which I think you will like. It is my sister's taste, and she is very proud of it."

He led the way along a broad passage or corridor, hung with large paintings—for so they seemed to me—with a heavy curtain between each.

"These are very fine paintings," I remarked, admiring a large sea-piece. The colouring was very fine, and it seemed to be worked out to the minutest detail.

"These are not paintings, but photographs," he replied; "there are no such things as paintings now, coloured photographs have quite taken their place. I don't believe there has been a picture painted for the last fifty years; nobody would buy one if there was: these are far better."

They certainly were. You might have been looking through an open window at the view, so life-like it was.

"But these," he went on, "are comparatively old-fashioned — we have got them to even greater perfection than that. I must show you my picture gallery — it is well worth seeing — but we'll keep that for tomorrow; come along."

At the end of the corridor he ushered me into a room that I had never seen the like of before. I cannot do it justice in this description, I fear. To begin with, it was circular; the walls were of a colour shading off from a deep rose at the foot into pink at the top, the dome overhead being also of the latter colour, giving the whole room a warm, glowing tint. There was a thick round velvet mat in the middle of the floor, pink in the centre and getting darker towards the sides, while beyond that there was a margin of white marble. Couches of crimson velvet and white ivory were scattered about the room, and there was a most delightful odour of sweet violets all through the air.

Mr. Adams motioned me to a seat, and as I sat down a strange soft music seemed to fill the air.

"Ah!" I said, "this feels like the Arabian Knights."

"Now," said Mr. Adams, "how would you like to hear Marmaduke Kinmont, our famous comic actor. He is playing just now in London."

"Very well indeed," I replied; "but if he is there I don't quite understand how we are to listen to him. You're not humbugging, are you?"

"Not at all, my dear sir." He moved across the room towards two large curtains which hung down from the ceiling. On his touching a button, these parted, falling away one on each side, and left exposed a large dark sheet of glass about twelve feet square. I watched with interest to see what would

*On his touching a button, these parted, falling away one on each side,
and left exposed a large dark sheet of glass about twelve feet square.*

happen next. He touched another button, and at once
the sheet of glass (or mirror, as I afterwards found it
to be) was brilliantly lit up. A stage was represented
upon it, and several figures moving about. He again
touched a button, and the effect was miraculous. The
figures were now heard speaking—you could follow
their voices as if they were indeed as near as they
were represented to be.

"Wonderful!" I exclaimed, starting up. "How,
in the name of all that is impossible, do you manage this?"

He returned across the room and sat down; I followed suit.

"It requires some explanation," he said, "but we
will watch the play first."

It was a funny piece of a type familiar enough
even after the lapse of a century. One man, who was
going to run away with another man's wife, ran away
with his own by mistake, and she for her part also
thought all the while she was running away with quite
another person. The play was very well acted, and you
heard the laughter and applause of the audience as if

you were in the theatre yourself. I was glad, however, when it came to an end, as I was anxious to hear my friend's explanation.

"What do you think of it?" he asked.

"It is indeed wonderful," I replied, "but I would like to understand how it is managed."

"Well," he began, "in the first place, that is a mirror we were looking at. In the theatre in London there is a small mirror placed, which reflects all that happens on the stage. In the theatre in this town there is also a small mirror, connected by a specially prepared wire (the nature of which I despair of making you understand in the present state of your knowledge) with the mirror in London; and everything reflected on the one mirror is at once transmitted to the other, where it is again reflected on to a large mirror the same size as the stage in London, and just taking the place of the stage here. In the last transmission, however, there is a magnifying glass placed in front of the mirror, which makes all the figures life-size. For the sound the telephone, which I believe was in vogue in your day, but has been much altered and improved, is used; and the smallest sound in the one theatre is heard in the other as distinctly as in the first, even to the furthest off part of the gallery. This, which is a private one of my own—I have to pay a tax of two hundred pounds a year for it, by the way—is a reflection, so to speak, of the one in this town, and worked on the same principle; but, as you yourself see, it loses nothing through being second-hand, only it is on a slightly smaller scale."

"It is the most wonderful invention I have yet seen," I said, "though indeed each one to me seems more wonderful than the last."

"No doubt," he replied, "to you, being suddenly introduced to such startling innovations, they must seem strange. But to us they are nothing. We have been brought up with them, and think no more of them than you did of the telegraph, for instance. But come—it's getting late, we must be off to bed." And rising, he made his way to the door. I followed. When we were in the hall we stepped on to the lift—not the one we went down on, but another situated at the other side of the hall, which also worked between two pillars. At once we were on the floor above. He showed me to my room—the one I had dressed in—said I would find everything I wanted in it, explained how to fasten the door and turn off the light, and wishing me good-night, left me.

"Well," I thought, "this has been a most eventful day. The year 2000, is it? I wonder if I'll be back in 1892 to-morrow, or moved on perhaps another century or so. That chap Adams isn't half a bad fellow, anyhow. Wonder what kind of a game he plays? Humph—going to teach me a thing or two, is he? We'll see about that." And so musing I took off my clothes, turned out the light, and got into bed. No sooner was my head on the pillow than I was fast asleep.

CHAPTER IV.

WE HAVE BREAKFAST — TUBULAR RAILWAYS — DECIDE ON
ST. ANDREWS — NEW COINAGE — THE TUB —
FAST TRAVELLING.

When I woke next morning the sun was shining in at my window. At first I wasn't very sure where I was; but gradually the events of yesterday began to dawn upon me. I took a furtive look round the room. It was all right—there were my clothes lying where I put them, and there was that patent bath I nearly lost my life in. It evidently had not been a dream.

53

I got up and dressed, taking pretty good care to keep well out of reach of that confounded bath, and hearing what I supposed was the breakfast gong, made my way—I was just going to say downstairs— out into the hall and down the lift. My host met me in the hall below.

"Good morning," he said; "how are you to-day? I was rather doubtful about seeing you this morning; I thought perhaps you would be in another trance."

"Oh, I'm all right," I replied; "I never felt better in my life: I don't intend to sleep for a hundred years every time I go to bed. I would very soon arrive at the end of the world, and then they wouldn't know what to do with me."

He ushered me into the breakfast-room, the walls of which were canary colour, shading off to a paler yellow still. On a table in the centre of the room breakfast was set, while on another table at the window were laid out all the morning papers.

"Now," said Mr. Adams, when we had begun breakfast, "what green would you like to play on?"

"It's all one to me," I answered—"whichever is the most convenient for you."

"They are all equally convenient," he replied, "from Thurso to Penzance."

"But I thought you were going to play to-day," I said; "and it would take a day to get to either of those places, wouldn't it?"

He laughed.

"My good friend," he said, still smiling, "you forget you are in the year 2000, and can travel from one end of Great Britain to the other in half an hour. If you cared, we could even play a round on both of the greens I mentioned."

"What, then, may I ask, is your motive-power now? You could not get that speed out of an engine worked by steam."

"Electricity," he replied, briefly—"tubular railways. All the lines are underground. But you will soon see for yourself. Have you settled what green you would like to play on?"

"Well," I said, "if I am to have my choice, what do you say to St. Andrews—if it's still in existence, that is to say?"

"St. Andrews, then, be it," he said, rising, as we finished breakfast.

"Look here," I said, "before we go any further, do your friends know about my lying in that trance all that time?"

"Yes," he answered, "some of them do, and they will be very much interested when they see you. And the doctors, too, who examined you—we must let them know."

"I would much rather you did not," I said—"at least for a little, till I get used to it. I don't exactly like the idea of being made a show of. You can introduce me as a friend or far-off cousin, can't you?"

"Very well, just as you like; but you know it must come out some time. In about two months it will be time for the doctors to come here in order to examine you again."

"Oh," I replied, "I don't mind after a bit, when the strangeness wears off; only at first, you know . . ."

"Right you are," he said; "for the present you are a distant connection. But we must start if we want to have a round at St. Andrews this morning. Come along, we have just time to catch the 'tub.'"

This was the contraction by which, as I found, the carriages in the tubular railway were familiarly styled.

We got on our hats—or caps, I should rather call them—and hurried out. Tall hats, I am glad to be able to inform you, are quite out of date in the year 2000. How the men in the nineteenth century could put up with them was always a mystery to me. They all, without exception, said they hated them; yet they always went on wearing them. I owned one, I have to admit, but luckily never had to put it on except to go to funerals. Indeed, it got so associated in my mind with funerals, that, if ever I wanted to feel sad, I just put it on and took a walk. Before I had gone half a dozen yards I was as sad as need be. You know the saddest time you ever had?—well, as sad as that.

We hadn't gone very far when my companion turned into a large, handsome building, where he at once approached a turnstile sort of arrangement, put a coin into a slit in the wall, and went through. He gave me a coin of the period, of the value of five shillings, and I followed his example.

The coinage was quite altered and much simpler. The decimal system was used; ten pence made one shilling, and ten shillings made one pound.

We were now in a small round room, which, as soon as we entered, descended a short distance, and deposited us in a long-shaped chamber brilliantly lighted. In this we found some half-dozen other men sitting about, smoking and reading the papers. My companion seemed to be known to most of them, judging from the " 'Morning, Adams," with which he was greeted by several. Nodding a reply, he turned to an elderly gentleman who sat in a corner and entered into earnest conversation with him.

I now had leisure to examine my fellow-travellers. They all seemed to be men of middle age, but the hairless condition of all their faces made it difficult to guess their ages. They were all dressed in the same stuff as we were ourselves; but a variety of colours was to be seen, chiefly dark browns and greys, with caps to match.

As I sat watching the men of the twenty-first century curiously, a bell gave a sharp, clear ring, and

the lift again descended. Three men got out of it, and
two who had been sitting by themselves rose and
stepped in and ascended by it. I noticed at one end of
the room, in large letters, the word "Edinburgh."
"What will that mean?" I wondered; but the next
moment the name had disappeared. Mr. Adams now
came over and sat down beside me.

"How do you like this mode of travelling?"
he asked.

"Very well indeed," I answered; "but when do
we start?"

"Start?" he said: "we are almost there; that was
Edinburgh we passed a minute ago. Did you not
notice it?"

"Yes, I did," I replied; "I noticed the word
'Edinburgh' in big letters up there, but had no idea
what it meant. But do you mean we are flying along
just now? Why, I haven't felt a single motion since we
came in."

"Ah! You see the perfection we have brought
travelling to nowadays. But here we are," he said,
jumping up, and at the same time I noticed, on the

same place where I had seen "Edinburgh," the name "St. Andrews." The lift descending at the same time, we got into it along with two other men, and were at once transferred into a large hall.

CHAPTER V.

On entering the hall we moved across it into another not quite so large, in which there were a great many men hanging about.

"We must see if we can get you the loan of a set of clubs and a coat," said Adams, crossing the hall. He soon returned.

"It's all right," he said; "young Lawson is laid up just now, so you can have his clubs and his coat as well; it will just fit you; you're both much about the same make. Come along and we'll try it on."

We went into a long-shaped room with mirrors running down the centre of it, and boxes all round the sides. Mr. Adams went up to one of the boxes, and, opening it, produced a coat which he helped me on with. It fitted perfectly, and felt nice and easy to golf in. We went back into the hall and forward to a large window, at which most of the men were congregated. The reason was that the teeing ground was just in front, and on a large board facing the window was the name of the man whose turn it was to play. As soon as each name was put up on the board a voice just above the window called it out in loud, clear tones. This, I afterwards discovered, was not a human voice, but was produced by the phonograph and worked in conjunction with the board outside. At every change of name a little bell sounded.

I was struck with the amount of order and the quietness with which everything was carried out. No one was on the teeing ground except the player and

his opponent. Not even a caddie. On my remarking
upon this to my friend, he replied:

"Oh, yes, they have their caddies; there they go."

Two players had just driven off and were leaving
the teeing ground, and sure enough behind each followed what I supposed was the caddies Mr. Adams
spoke of; a perpendicular rod about four feet long,
supported on three wheels, the whole rather resem-
bling a small tricycle with a small mast stepped where
the saddle should have been. This rod was weighted
at the foot and hung on the wheels, so that it was
always perpendicular, however steep the gradient it
was going up or down. On this contrivance the clubs
were carried, and the players seemed to drag the
whole affair after them. It seemed to me a poor substitute for the good old-fashioned caddie, about
whom so many stories are told, and who were always
ready with advice, and good advice too. My
nineteenth-century memory recalled a lad who, one
morning, on each successive putting-green, showed
me the line to the hole by saying it lay "owre that
yelley fleur." I may mention that there was not a

It seemed to me a poor substitute for the good old-fashioned caddie,
about whom so many stories are told, and who were always ready
with advice, and good advice, too.

"yelley fleur" on the whole links; and that my friend
was *not* a teetotaler.

As we watched this couple and their queer
mechanical caddies the voice shouted "Walter
Adams," and simultaneously his name appeared on
the board outside.

"Come on," he said, "it's our turn."

We went down a broad flight of steps on to the
green. At the foot of the steps we were met by two
caddies—for I suppose I must give the things the old
name. They had come from immediately below the
room we had been in; but they didn't require to be
drawn or indeed worked in any way. They simply followed wherever we went, at a distance of twelve feet
or so, and regulated themselves to our pace, stopped
when we stopped, and so on. Their wheels shot out
spikes when necessary, so that they might not slip
going up steep bits, or through bunkers and places of
that kind. My friend explained that we had a sort of
magnet behind our jackets which attracted them, but
at the same time did not allow them to come nearer
than the twelve feet before mentioned. Of course you

could go up to them when they had stopped; but when you moved on they remained stationary until you were the twelve feet away, and not till then did they follow.

Each carried its clubs in an oblong box, where they lay with the heads exposed, as in my own time. I took out what I supposed was a driver. It was a very powerful weapon with a remarkably thin shaft, which, on closer inspection, turned out to be made of steel—indeed the head, too, was made of that metal. The shaft terminated in a little white disc, under glass, with figures on it and a hand like the face of a very small watch. There was another small disc on the sole of the club. This one was, however, quite plain. My friend, seeing my look of astonishment, said:

"Ah! I thought we would show you something new in the way of clubs. What do you think of that, eh?"

"It seems a wonderful weapon," I replied; "but what are all those dials for?"

"That one," he said, pointing to the one at the top of the shaft, "registers every stroke you take with the club. It is on every club, and as the strokes you have taken with each club are registered, the total of the set is your score for the round. At the end of the round your clubs are handed in to the secretary, who with his clerks counts the scores and awards the prize-money accordingly. You must understand that every day there is, so to speak, a competition. Every player pays five shillings before starting the round. This money is divided into two parts: one half goes to keep up the green, pay salaries, of which there are a good many, taxes, &c.; the other half goes in prize-money. There is one scratch prize and about six handicap. We have got handicapping as near perfection as possible, for you see we have a record of every round a man plays, and by taking his average from day to day, and from week to week, we soon arrive at his right figure. Every man keeps an account with the secretary, and at the end of the week draws his winnings, that is to say, if he has any. Some men make quite a good thing of it."

"You are very far advanced in golf, I see, as well as everything else. But what is this for?" I said, pointing to the dial on the sole of the club.

"Oh, that," he answered, "registers the length of your drive—at least, of your carry. The head is a wonderful little piece of mechanism, with about as much work in it as in a watch. You see the face is slightly detached from the rest of the head; it is fixed to it by an immense number of small springs, which indeed almost fill the head, so that the propelling power of the club is greater than could be got from the shaft alone. But we must start. I think that couple in front are far enough ahead. Is the grip all right?" he added, looking at me.

"It's rather thick," I replied, "but it will do, I think."

"Oh, we'll soon put that all right," he said. He took my club, and, screwing something at the top, reduced the grip. The balls, which didn't seem, judging from appearances, to have undergone any marked change, having been teed, my companion motioned me to drive.

I addressed myself to the ball, and in the middle of my swing a voice which seemed to come from close behind me called out "Fore," in a way that quite put me off, and made me top my ball.

"Sir," I said, turning quickly round to my companion, for he was the only other person on the ground, "it was *not* customary in my day to speak when a player was addressing himself to his ball, much less to shout 'Fore' in the middle of his swing."

Mr. Adams said nothing. He only smiled, and, taking a club, prepared to drive off. In the middle of his swing he again called out "Fore," much to my astonishment.

"Is this a new rule?" I asked him. "Must you always call 'Fore' in the middle of your swing?"

"I didn't call 'Fore,'" he answered, with a twinkle in his eye. I felt very much inclined to call him a liar, but restrained myself. We moved on, followed by our peculiar caddies. We were not long in coming to my ball which I had topped. I looked at it and then at my clubs. To tell the truth I was not very sure which one to take, some were of such curious shapes.

"That's your club," said Mr. Adams, taking from my set a club with a funny-looking oblong sort of head. It seemed to have been put on the wrong way, and you hit with its nose. A small bit also projected behind, making it something like a polo-stick on a small scale. I took this weapon, and again, in the middle of my swing, there came a shout of "Fore," which of course gave me such a start that I missed my shot once more. I fairly lost my temper this time.

"What do you mean by trying to put me off in this manner?" I shouted. "If that's the way you win your golf matches nowadays, the less I know of golf in the year 2000 the better."

"Take it easy," Adams replied, with another laugh, "and I'll explain."

"Explain!" I said; "I don't see what there is to explain."

"That long sleep of yours has evidently not destroyed your temper," he said, with a quiet smile; "but as I said before, I did not call 'Fore'; in fact, I believe it's years since I called 'Fore' while golfing. You take a swing without hitting the ball; watch me instead, and see if I speak."

I did so; and sure enough the voice again shouted "Fore"; but it evidently wasn't my companion's doing, as his lips had remained tightly closed.

Somehow the sound seemed to come actually from myself. I was more puzzled than ever. Adams burst out laughing at my look of amazement.

"My dear fellow," he said, still laughing, "it's your jacket. Another new invention for you. The sound comes from under your arms when you swing. It acts like a concertina: draws the air in when you take the club back, and when you bring the club down out comes the voice."

"Well," I said, "you have certainly brought golf to a nice pass. The clubs keep their own score; your jacket shouts 'Fore,' your caddie keeps his mouth shut—everything seems to be turned topsy-turvy. You ought to have an invention for swinging the club, and all you would have to do would be to walk round smoking your pipe and superintending operations."

"Oh, it's not quite so bad as that yet," he answered; "but there's no saying what it will come to."

The course at St. Andrews was not what it was in my day. All the whins had disappeared, and we played, going out, along by the sea, and came in on the old course, though it had been entirely re-planned. I need not go over the round: suffice it to say I 'got my licks'—I won't tell you by how many. There were still eighteen holes in the round, though much longer ones than I had been accustomed to, and I wasn't sorry to get to the last. But like every golfer, I must have excuses for my bad play. To begin with, that *beastly* jacket was one—and a very good one—it was always putting me off. My companion soothingly explained that it might be some little time ere I got used to it; and that when I once did so I would never notice the sound. He said that, for his own part, sometimes he never even heard it. I thought to myself it wouldn't be a bad plan at first to stuff one's ears with cotton wool or something of that sort to deaden the sound.

And the clubs—a queerer collection I never saw. As I said before, they were all made in one piece, and were of steel. The faces all protruded about half an inch beyond the place where the shaft and head met. The heads were very small, which gave the clubs the appearance of hammers, and some looked as if you could reverse them and play left-handed. Of course, though the clubs were entirely of steel, they were painted so that they did not look so very unlike the old tools. There were no irons in the set—at least, what nineteenth-century people understand as irons. Golfers seemed to have gone back to the old baffy in a sort of way. The heads of the clubs they played approaches with were larger, the faces very much laid back, and slanting diagonally across the head. To look at these you would imagine you would slice everything. My companion showed me how to use them in order to put a cut on the ball and stop it. He himself did it wonderfully, laying a ball quite dead if he chose. But the niblick was the funniest of the lot. It had a double head, and when you swung it, it revolved like the paddle-wheel of a steamboat, only very much faster. You addressed the ball with the one head, while the other came up behind the shaft, it being of course quite stationary. As soon as you swung the club the two heads began to revolve—the opposite way from a paddle-wheel, of course—and threw the ball out of the bunker, with no end of sand. You had to look out for your eyes if there was any wind.

I must not forget the balls—they are quite worthy of description. To all appearance, as I have said, they were the same as we used in '92; but though innocent enough to look at, they had more work in them than even the heads of the clubs. In the centre of the ball was a small chamber of compressed air; outside that was a rim of some hard substance like gutta-percha, about a quarter of an inch thick; then came the shell of the ball, which was made up of oblong little blocks, of the same hard, white substance before mentioned. These blocks were each separate, and fixed to the inside layer by strong springs—four springs to every single square—crossing each other. When they were all fixed on the ball quite resembled one of the old-fashioned gutties. Even handling them you did not detect the difference, and the flying power was extraordinary.

So you see that with all those new inventions taken into account, it was hardly to be expected I could play much of a game to start with. Adams *had* taught me a thing or two after all, but I determined to get into form, accustom myself to the new clubs, and see if I couldn't turn the tables on him. "It's not the clubs that make the golfer, after all," I said to myself, consolingly.

Chapter VI.

On going round the green I had noticed at regular intervals, on both sides of the course, very long, perpendicular poles, that looked about four hundred feet or so high. On asking my companion what they were used for, he replied:

"Ah, that will give you some idea to what lengths we have brought golf. You observe there is a double row of poles, one on each side of the course.

Between those two rows a mirror is suspended hori-
zontally at the height of four hundred and fifty feet,
covering the whole length of the green. Of course it
does not require to be the breadth of the course; a
strip down the centre serves the purpose. The glass is
only put up when an important match is in progress.
Everything going on on the green is then reflected
overhead; in the club-house, at the first hole, there is
a small mirror, so placed that it reflects what is in the
large mirror overhead, at any point you choose. Thus,
when a match starts, the small mirror is almost horizontal, the players being so close, and being first
reflected to the mirror above and then back again on
to the small one. As the players get further off—of
course we are only following one couple or foursome,
as the case may be—the small mirror gradually tilts
up, till, when the players are at the furthest distance
from the start, it is at an angle of about eighty
degrees. Then gradually, as the players return, the
angle gets smaller, till the glass resumes its former
almost horizontal position. You observe it has been
following the reflection of the players all this time.

It is worked by a female, who has full charge of it,
and has to be very careful in the following of the
match. This small mirror is connected by a wire, specially prepared, as in the case of the theatre wires, to
a mirror in London, we will say, though of course it
can be, and sometimes is, connected with a thousand
different mirrors, on the same principle as those theatre ones which I showed you last night. The figures
are seen life-size, walking along and taking their
shots; indeed, you see them from the first drive off,
till they hole out the last putt; and people in London
and all the large towns can watch a golf match going
on here. They pay two shillings, take a seat as if they
were at a theatre, and watch the reflection on their
own special mirrors, wherever they may be. Of course
they don't hear anything. But you mustn't think every
golfing green has this contrivance; it is confined to
only a very few, I think about fifty or so, and they play
the big matches only on those."

"By Jove!" I said, "that seems almost a fable; but
I would like to be in London and watch a match
played here."

It is worked by female, who has full charge of it, and has to be very careful in the following of the match. This small mirror is connected by a wire . . . to a mirror in London. . . .

"Nothing easier," he answered; "next big match that comes off we'll go to London and have front seats."

As we had finished the round, we went back to the club.

"You'll be thirsty," said Adams; "at least I am. What will you drink?"

"I'll have a whisky and potash," I answered; "at least if there is still such a drink in existence."

"Ah," he said, "we have been able to improve upon a lot of your old-fashioned ways; but the Auld Kirk has stood its ground. It was the drink of the past, it is the drink of the present, and it will be the drink of the future. As long as there are golfers to drink it, there will be distillers to make it."

Going up to the side of the room, round which a ledge ran, about three feet from the floor, he put a coin in a slot and produced tumblers of whisky and potash—one for himself and one for me.

As we seated ourselves and were filling our pipes—I was glad to see that they still smoked pipes—

one of the men whom I had seen sitting at the window came up and accosted my companion.

"How are you, Adams?" he said. "Had a good round?"

"Oh, fairly," Adams replied. "I was just going round with my friend, Mr. Gibson. Let me introduce you two—Mr. Gibson, Mr. White. He has not been playing for some time past, having been laid up."

I bowed.

"I hope it has been nothing serious, Mr. Gibson," said Mr. White, bowing also.

"Oh, no," I replied, smiling. "I have been troubled with somnolence, and have been under medical treatment for some time" (some considerable time, I thought to myself), "so have got rather out of form. But a round or two will put me all right again, I hope. The greens are in first-rate order."

"Yes," said Mr. White, "I have seldom seen them looking better. What do you think of the big match next week?"

"What match is that?" I asked. I must take care not to betray ignorance, I thought to myself.

"Why, the match against the Cape of Good Hope," he answered. "It is played every year between teams of twenty men a-side; last year it was played at the Cape. The Scotchmen have won every time since the institution of the match, but I believe the Cape players are very strong this year, and intend to give us a tussle for it."

"A very interesting match," I said. "I suppose it is played by holes?"

"Yes," he replied. "We had a very close shave for the International Championship last year; but I suppose you know all that."

"No, I don't," I answered. "You see I have been kept very quiet for some time, and you people have got rather ahead of me." — There was more truth in this than he imagined. — "But tell me about it."

"Oh, there's not much to tell," he went on. "In the final with Canada — it is played in foursomes, you know — we only managed to win by one hole, after being all square and one to play. The excitement over that last hole through the whole country was something frightful. Jack Dornoch, who holed a long putt at the finish and won the match, was knighted, and got a pension of a thousand a year for life."

"He's a wonderful player, Dornoch," broke in Adams. "What is the latest betting about his match with the American?"

"Five to four on Dornoch, I believe," said White; "but Michigan" (that was the American, I supposed) "is a tremendous player, if all accounts be true. The game will be well worth seeing—I'll watch it in London, I think. It's a pity they hadn't arranged to play it in this country. I've never played on any American greens myself, though I suppose they are very good."

Watch it in London, I thought, and it to be played in America! Then I recollected the mirrors, and wondered if it could be possible to transmit the whole match through the ocean.

"I wonder," I said, turning to White, "what a golfer of a century ago would say were he to rise from his grave and see the way you play golf now."

"I expect he would be a little surprised, to say the least of it," said White.

"I expect he would," I admitted, with a wink to Adams. "They thought they knew everything about golf, while, indeed, they knew nothing or next to nothing. It was in its infancy, and you won't have got it to perfection until you have a machine for walking round the green and swinging the club, while you sit here and manage it."

"Well, I don't think it will ever be so bad as that," said White, "though certainly there have been a tremendous number of improvements in the last hundred years. Talking of improvements," he went on, "I see that experiment of Dr. Fawcett's has been a complete success. It will be a great thing now to have the weather under complete control. If we could only manage the wind."

The weather under complete control! I thought— the man must be mad! What *can* this invention be?

"Ah, yes," said Adams, throwing a warning glance in my direction, "it will be a great thing. I thought it would come, it was an easy matter to bring the rain, but it was no joke when you could not get it turned off. This will simplify matters very much."

"I must be going, though," said White, rising. "We will have a game some day, I hope, Mr. Gibson."

"I will be very happy," I answered; "but I must get into form first."

"Well, we will arrange later on. Good-bye for the present."

So saying, he left us and made his way across the hall.

When we were alone I turned to Adams.

"What, in the name of all that's wonderful, do you mean by controlling the weather?" I said.

"Ah," he said, "I was afraid White would notice your look of astonishment. It is a great discovery. Scattered about the country are very high towers, about two thousand feet high, made of steel: some are placed on mountains, so that they do not require to be quite so high. When we want rain, from the top of this tower are shot up balls of some kind of chemical, which explode, and never fail to bring rain; in about half an hour it comes down in torrents; but we were never able to stop it; sometimes it would just be a shower, at other times it went on for days, and did more harm than good; but, as you heard White say, they have discovered something to stop the rain and drive away the clouds. I read something about it lately. It is a ball of some other chemical which also explodes, but acts in the reverse way, stopping the rain and dispersing the clouds. So now we will be able to suit ourselves with our weather. For a big match we'll have the greens well watered beforehand, and a fine day to play the match on. There are only about a dozen of these towers in Great Britain. One takes in a radius of sixty miles or so."

"Well," I could only say, "I'm not going to be surprised at anything more you tell me after that. But do you really mean that you can turn rain off and on at will?"

"Undoubtedly," he replied. "I don't think any of your nineteenth-century people ever dreamt of *that.*"

"No, I'm certain none of them did," I replied; "but look here, White was saying something about an International Championship. What did he mean?"

"That is a great annual match, perhaps the greatest of the year. Each country is represented by four players, and it is played in foursomes by holes. There were, I think, close on twenty different countries entered last year, and the finish was very exciting, as White said. Since the institution of the match Scotland has won no less than twenty-seven times, England eleven, while Canada and Australia have each won once."

"I'm glad to see Scotland still takes the lead as far as golf is concerned," I answered.

"Yes, indeed," said Adams, rising. "Now, if you have finished your drink, we had better go. We'll get back in plenty of time for dinner."

We moved across the hall, and Adams putting a coin in the slot, we were once more back in the train or "tub." We had no sooner taken our seats, it seemed to me, than the lift came down again; but as my companion did not move, I concluded it wasn't our station, and on looking at the wall again, I saw "Edinburgh" in large letters. I wondered why we only stopped at Edinburgh, but on my asking Adams he explained that the trains ran every five minutes, and each one had a different set of stations to stop at.

There were time-tables, of course; but he was so well up in all the trains, having to use them so much, that he did not require to refer to one. As he finished his explanation we arrived at our station, and, ascending in the lift, were once more in the open air.

In going along the street I noticed that we never saw any ladies walking about; in fact, I had not seen a female of any kind, which struck me as rather peculiar. I thought that perhaps, among other improvements, they had got the ladies to stay at home; however, I did not remark on this to my companion.

While walking along I began to think about how I was to live. I could not go on spunging on Adams, though he seemed to take it quite as a matter of course. That was out of the question. Therefore I explained my predicament to my friend. To my surprise, he told me that a sum of money had been invested in my name by my relations, in case I ever came to life again, and that this had been accumulating ever since. In the event of my death, while lying in the trance, the money was to have gone to found a mission station at the North Pole, or perhaps the South Pole—I am not sure which, and don't greatly care. I was not dependent on Adams's generosity after all, and the news made me feel much more comfortable. Adams would not hear of me leaving him, however; I was to consider myself his guest for the present, till I had time to look about me and get used to everything.

Before I could get my money it seemed that I would require doctors' certificates and a declaration from Mr. Adams that I was the so-called A. J. Gibson come to life again. Now, as I said before, I did not want to make a show of myself quite yet. But I'll have to do it soon in order to get the cash, I mused, for I don't suppose they can get on even nowadays without filthy lucre.

Chapter VII.

How they cross the Atlantic — What the ladies of
2000 do — Miss Adams — Has the female sex degenerated? —
The picture gallery — Miss Adams again; a little too much
of her this time.

When we had arrived home I made my way to my
bedroom, had a wash, and changed my clothes.
Adams, you know, had let me into the secret of the
wardrobe. Then I went down to the morning-room,
where we had had breakfast. There were a lot of
papers lying about, and I took up one to pass the
time. The first thing that caught my eye was a head-
ing, "A Fast Trip to America." I wonder what they have

reduced the Atlantic record to now, I thought; I expect it will almost be under the five days. You can judge of my astonishment when I read:

"The fastest trip yet made to America by the Transatlantic Tubular Railway was achieved yesterday. The 10 o'clock car from London arrived at New York at 12:32, thus taking only two hours and thirty-two minutes, and beating the last record by thirteen minutes. The stoppage at the half-way station was abolished, which saved some minutes. It will be some time before this record is broken."

"So I should expect," I said to myself, laying down the papers as Adams joined me.

"Been amusing yourself with the papers?" he said.

"Yes," I replied. "I see they have been making a very fast trip to America."

"Oh, they are always at that," he answered; "anything under three hours is good."

"But, by Jove, I would not like to risk myself for three hours under the Atlantic," I said. "Is that tubular railway quite safe?"

"Safe?—yes, there has not been an accident since it started. The world is a very small place now. You can go right round it in a day, and feel as if you had never left your own house. What do you think of that?"

"Well, I told you I was not going to be surprised at anything more. So I'm not. I won't be astonished even if you inform me you take a trip to the moon occasionally for change of air. But, I forgot, they've got no air there, have they?"

"No, we've not got that length," he replied, "we'll leave that for another generation or two. The legacy left in your own day for that purpose hasn't been claimed yet. By the by, my sister has come home. I saw her and explained about you. She is quite agreeable to let you remain incog. for the present, but is very anxious to see you. You mustn't be surprised when you see her, however; for women, I must tell you, don't dress as they did in your days, but clothe themselves just as we men do. You can't tell the difference between the sexes at a glance, as in your day."

"That will account for my not seeing any ladies, as I thought, in the street."

"Yes, that's it, you would not be able to distinguish them from men; and, in fact, in a business capacity, they are on an equality with men. More than half of all our eminent lawyers, ministers, and doctors are women; there are more women in Parliament than men, and in the public offices, such as banks, &c., all the clerks are women. There is not such a thing as a male clerk now. All we men have got to do is to play golf, while the women do all the work."

"What!" I cried, slapping my knee, "the dream of my former existence come true! I am, indeed, a lucky man to see it. The women working while the men play golf! Splendid! The world is evidently getting things ship-shape. But you have the nineteenth century to thank for it. 'Twas we first began to give golf its proper position as a chief end of man; for generations it has been developing, and you now reap the fruits. Oh, how I would like to wake up some of my old chums! I know a few who would appreciate the arrangement."

"Come along in the meantime," said Adams, with a smile at my enthusiasm, "and I will introduce you to my sister."

We went up to what I may call the pink drawing-room. Seated at a table, writing, we found what I took to be another man. She—for I rightly concluded this was my host's sister—rose on our approach.

"Allow me to introduce you to my sister, Mr. Gibson," said my companion.

She held out her hand.

"I am very pleased to see you once more in the full possession of all your faculties, Mr. Gibson. Yours has, indeed, been a wonderful case. We have been so accustomed to see you lying as if you were dead. In fact, I used to think you were really dead, in spite of what the doctors said; but I am very glad to see you restored to health instead. How do you like the way we live now?"

"You are very kind, Miss Adams," I said. "I am charmed with everything I either hear or see in this wonderful age. In my days we did not live as it seems to me now. And yet they were happy days too; the memory of some of them I would not exchange for anything in this new and wonderful world."

"Ah, true!" she replied. "Old associations cling to one. Yours has been a unique experience, to have lived in two ages. And yours was a queer old humdrum world compared with this."

"Indeed, I can assure you," I said, "we did not consider it a queer old humdrum world, but quite the reverse. Who knows but that in another hundred years or so you too will be out of date? But I am very pleased with the position the ladies occupy now. I was always a women's rights man. I used to say, if they wanted to take upon them a share in matters we thought they knew nothing about, and so relieve us of our responsibilities, why, let 'em. Then we shall have all the more leisure for golf and amusement. Why should their sweet voices not be heard in public, and if they were allowed to speak more in public, they might take it into their contrary little heads to speak less in private. You must not think me rude though," I added, "it's an old-world argument. The ladies of the present day are all that is charming, I am sure; even this wonderful age cannot change that."

She smiled.

"That is an old-world compliment," she said; "men do not pay compliments now-a-days, they have no time, or, rather, the women have none to spare for listening to them. And you are a golfer? My brother will be able to show you plenty that will interest you in that line. It is all the men can employ themselves with—golf, golf, golf, is the one cry."

"Ah," I said, "they play golf in a way that was never even dreamt of in my day. The clubs quite confuse me, and the scoring is extraordinary. And the caddies!—"

She held up her hands in protest—the gesture at least was feminine.

"Ah," she said; "there it begins. And I have such a quantity of work to get through before dinner!" Therewith she withdrew—rather abruptly I thought.

Adams apologised, becomingly, speaking of his sister at the same time with a very deferential air, and in quite a tone of pride.

"That is an old-world compliment," she said; "men do not pay compliments now-a-days, they have no time, or, rather, the women have none to spare for listening to them."

"She is a member of Parliament, you see, and a very rising one too. Women make very good legislators but for one thing, and that is, for a paltry victory over a rival, or to pay off a private spite, they would let the country go to the dogs. Though every generation produces cleverer women than the last, that narrow-minded rivalry or jealousy seems to be ingrained in the sex, and though they improve in other respects, in that respect they get worse; it seems to get intensified as the race gets older. For that reason few ladies get into the Cabinet, and we have never yet had a female Prime Minister; though, to be sure, there is a great talk that the next Prime Minister will be a woman. However, we men don't take much interest in these things; we leave the ladies to fight it out among themselves, and they don't betray our trust, they *do* fight it out."

"From what you have said," I replied, "it seems to me that the female sex, if you will excuse me saying so, has degenerated. The ladies in my day did not bother themselves about politics—though, to be sure, they were all great home rulers. Home was their kingdom, and right well they used to govern it. They shared our joys and sorrows; in success, they were the first we turned to; in adversity, we went to them. What would a sick room have been without a woman to anticipate our every want, to smooth the pillow, and to give us a feeling of security that what could be done would be done? From the time they bring us into the world till we leave it they look after us; and after our course is run, who is it but a woman who performs those last sad offices, and leaves us at rest for ever?" And as I finished I remembered one, one whom I had loved; ah, me, she must have died about seventy years ago, and perhaps a grandmother for all I know.

"Ah, well," he added, "I daresay it strikes you women have changed scarcely for the better. Yet, do you know, from their point of view, it is *we* who have degenerated! and" (this was said with a sigh) "we certainly are no longer the lords of creation that you were in your generation, I can assure you."

Just then the gong sounded, and with an air which let me see that the change of subject was not altogether unpleasant.

"Ah," said Adams, "there is dinner at last. I have no doubt you will be quite ready for it—St. Andrews air was always a good appetiser."

We went down to the dining-room, and fed in the same style as before. They may invent a new way of bringing the food to you, I reflected, as the dishes came and went, but they can't invent a new way of eating it.

After dinner we had a look at my host's pictures—photographs rather—elaborate productions, which Adams descanted on at length, though it needed not that to compel my admiration. Among the portraits were, what seemed to me, most novel and ingenious curiosities. There was, for instance, a life-size figure of a golfer playing a shot. As we looked he was addressing himself to the ball. He looked up once and then swung his club, and the ball at the same moment disappeared. No sooner was the one swing over than he began another. That was a likeness of Peter Gullane, a famous golfer of the period, my host told me.

"It is certainly a very fine picture," I said, "I could spend days in this wonderful gallery of yours."

"But come along," said Adams, "my sister will think we are lost; you can come back here whenever you like; the whole house, you know, is at your disposal."

Afterwards we went along to the pink room, where we found Miss Adams again engaged in writing.

"What do you think of the pictures?" she asked.

"They are splendid," I answered; "I never even dreamt that photography could be brought to such perfection. You must have thought us almost savages, who lived in that barbarous nineteenth century."

"Not at all," she replied. "As much credit is due to you as to us. You laid the foundation stones, we have only continued the building. Some think that once the progression is completed, and 'perfection' written above the door, the world will cease. But it is not by new inventions we shall get that perfection. We want the perfection of the mind and the body, as well as of the things that minister to the mind and the body; and while the men will think of nothing but golf, how can it be done? We women are always trying to awaken them to a sense of their responsibilities. They were not put into this world to play golf, though, I believe, they think so."

"Well," said Adams, breaking in, "I, for one, don't want the world to cease, and I think we're doing you a service in keeping it going. For if you don't think you'll get what you call perfection—though as to what that is I don't think you seem very clear yourself—till we stop golf, then I think the world will go on for some considerable time. And as for the next world, the savage red man of the prairie looked forward to his happy hunting ground. Why should the savage white man not look forward to his happy golfing ground?"

"Ah," she said, "that is well said. The savage white man! You *are* savages, and Golf is the god you worship. Yet what does he do for you but wreck your tempers? When you have played a bad game and lost the match, you come home and sulk and sulk till you have played a good one and got yourself in a good humour. I would not worship such a god—one day all smiles and the next all frowns; and you poor weak deluded men worship on. When he frowns to-day you hope he will smile to-morrow. I pity you."

"But do ladies not play golf now?" I ventured to interpose. "In my time they were as keen about it as the men, and some of them were very good players."

"*No*, Mr. Gibson," replied Miss Adams, "the ladies of to-day *do not* play golf. They have more to do. Their time is taken up in discharging the duties that the men leave undone. *We* find there is more in life than golf."

"Ah, well," her brother interrupted, "it's very kind of you to pity our sad state, but I'm afraid it's lost upon us. But Gibson here is looking sleepy. You must be tired," he added, turning to me, "after that round of St. Andrews, and you know you have not been used to much exertion lately. Let's retire."

"I do feel sleepy," I admitted; and with a "good-night" to Miss Adams and her brother I made my way to my room.

Humph, I thought to myself, I don't think that Miss Adams improves on acquaintance. Doesn't seem as if we'd get on. I think I'll avoid her in

future. A little of her goes a very long way. And thus
meditating I found myself in bed, and was soon fast
asleep dreaming of men coming out of pictures and
playing golf, and somebody always yelling "fore" in
my ear.

CHAPTER VIII.

The next morning I was awakened by Adams rushing into my room.

"What, not up yet!" he cried. "Out of that at once! I've just been speaking to White, that fellow we saw yesterday, and he wants us to meet him at Golfton at eleven to play a foursome. What do you say?"

"The very thing," I replied. "I used to be very fond of Golfton, and would like very much to see it now. I expect it has changed a good deal, though."

"Yes, it has," he said. "But hurry up, we have not too much time, and I must see about getting you clubs. You must have a set of your own. I'll look after that just now. When you're ready, come down, and I'll have some looked out for you to choose from"; and with that he disappeared out of the patent door.

"Golfton," I said to myself, "that's splendid. I wonder how the old place will be looking after a hundred years of changes. The old landmarks will be the same, but all the faces will be new. Ay, ay, that's a penalty I've got to pay for living a hundred years beyond my time."

When I had finished dressing—I again took good care to keep well out of reach of that bath, for though if it be true that burnt children dread the fire, it is equally certain that half-drowned men dread the water—I went down, down, down, down—where? down the lift—ay, that's it, it's very difficult remembering not to say downstairs—and into the morning-room, where Adams, as good as his word, was surrounded by dozens of new patent golf-clubs.

"Ah, here you are," he said, as I entered. "I think we'll be able to find something here that will suit you."

"I don't know much about those clubs of yours, though," I replied. "I'll have to rely more on your judgment than on my own."

He first picked out a driver, and after looking at several, I fixed upon one. It seemed to suit me because the feel of it was quite like the old wooden clubs I was accustomed to. I think I described the club before with its self-registering dial, &c. I said before there were no so-called iron clubs in use— except, of course, the revolving niblick. The nearest approach to one was a club with a very small head, something like our old driving mashy, but with a double face. Between the faces were placed all sorts of springs, &c., making it look more like the inside of a watch than aught else.

We picked six clubs—by the way, they evidently did not go in for the great sheaf of clubs so common in my day, but we carried one or two extra heads in case of accidents. The shaft fitted into a socket at the neck with a spring, or catch, which was tightened by screwing something at the other end of the shaft. It had to be carefully done, as the apparatus for scoring was carried from the head up the shaft.

Adams told me that some time ago there was a great move to do away with even the patent caddie, and carry the heads loose, taking only one shaft round with you, to fit all the heads; but this was found to be impracticable, as the heads were difficult to carry. Time, too, was put off in changing; for you could not, of course, change when walking between the shots, having to see how your ball was lying ere you knew what head you required. So that idea exploded.

When we had settled on the clubs—and a queer collection they were, too—Adams proposed breakfast, and we sat down. I was always a great hand at breakfast, especially with a big day's golf before me. Many's the last extra slice of toast I've put down after being quite satisfied, and felt the benefit of when about three holes from home, seeing my opponent going a little off, while I had plenty of "back" left, thanks to that last slice. At lunch, too, always make a good meal, say I, such as a couple of good chops or a steak, for choice, with a pint of beer to wash it down. You feel twice the man after it, and there's no funk in you. You go for everything, and everything—or nearly everything—comes off. You put every putt at the back of the hole, and a good many of them find the bottom. The man, on the other hand, who has lunched on two wine biscuits and a bottle of potash, to keep his nerves all right, as he thinks, tries to creep round bunkers, and gets into them (serves him right, too); his putts are never up, and consequently, according to that time-honoured maxim, never in. No, no. If you want to play golf, *feed*. Nor is there any necessity to forget the drink—in moderation, of course, or you'll be seeing stimies. If you don't feed the engine with fuel, you can't expect to get any work out of it.

But I must return to my subject, since I did not start out to give a lecture on "What food to eat, and how to eat it." I never attended one myself, never thought I required to. I fancied I knew pretty well *what* to eat, and as for *how to*—well, it would be a decided waste of time for any doctor to teach *me* that. There I am again, drivelling away about what's got nothing to do with this biography. No, no; it's not a biography. History, is it? No, it's not a history either. Well, never mind what it is. These are points you can settle for yourselves, gentle reader. I suppose, by the way, you *are* gentle, though why I should suppose so, I don't know, only I've always heard readers talked about as gentle, and now when I come to think of it, when I'm reading a book I do feel gentle. You see I'm sitting in an armchair over the fire, I've had a good dinner, and my pipe is going—that's always when I read books—and I do feel gentle, I wouldn't harm a fly; and if anybody brought in a collection book in aid of a home for idiotic authors, I would head a new page. So you see when you read this I expect you to be gentle, at least try and look gentle, and don't shy the book to the other end of the room with a muttered "D—d trash." There now, you were just going to do it; but bear with me a little longer and I'll try and behave better.

On this occasion, at all events, I made a capital

breakfast. Adams, between mouthfuls, gave me scraps of news—golfing news, of course, for the paper he had stuck up in front of him contained very little else.

Miss Adams did not breakfast with us, for which I was not very sorry. Her brother explained that she breakfasted early and was away to London. I uttered a secret prayer that she would stop there. That kind of female—well, I don't mind reading about them, but when it comes to a personal interview—I'd rather not. And she was just a little too large an order for me.

"That man Michigan seems to be in great form," said Adams, looking up from the paper which he was reading. "I see he has broken another record. The Yankees think no end of him; but I intend to back our man. It'll be a good match, though. We'll see it in London, and then you'll find how useful the mirrors are."

"I should like to see it," I replied; "but don't you think it's about time to be starting for Golfton."

"By Jove! You're right," he said, jumping up. "We'll have to hurry, and you haven't got your jacket yet. Come on."

He tore out of the room, and I followed. We jumped into the lift, and were at once on the floor above. He rushed into my room, opened the wardrobe, and produced a jacket.

"Here you are," he said. "Allow me."

"Is that that patent 'fore' jacket?" I asked. "Because if so, I would rather be without one. It always puts me off, and I know I'll never get used to it."

"Oh, but you must," he answered. "Every golfer has to wear one: it is a rule. There is a heavy fine if a man is found playing without one."

"If I must, I suppose I must," I replied, getting into it. "But if you take my advice you will not be on my side to-day. I'll never be able to hit a shot with the confounded thing, what between expecting and listening for the shout, and then the shout itself."

At last we got started, I armed with my new clubs and my jacket, *à la* concertina. We went into the same building as on the preceding day; repeated the operation of putting a coin in the slot, and descended into a room similar to the one of yesterday. The coin,

I noticed, was the same as I had used in the trip to St. Andrews, and on my making this observation to Adams, he explained that they had only one fare, which was five shillings, and for that you could travel as far as you liked. If you wanted to travel a few miles you had to pay the same fare as you would were you to travel from one end of Great Britain to the other. It was automatic. You could not get into the train without first paying your fare. There were no porters or officials, or if there were I never saw any.

During the journey we made two stops, which I had come to recognise by seeing names appear on the wall, and the lift come down for passengers to get in and out. The last name just seemed to have disappeared, and I was looking at the place in the wall wondering what the next would be, when "Golfton" was signalled.

Chapter IX.

The new putter — Golfton in the year 2000 — We have a round — And win the match — The electric shoot — Another talk with Miss Adams — She proves too many for me.

"Ah, here we are!" said Adams, rising. "I wonder if White has arrived!"

We ascended by the lift into a large hall, much the same as that at St. Andrews, and on crossing it found ourselves in a smaller one, where a crowd of men were standing round a window. One of them, whom I recognised as the Mr. White we had met on the previous day, came forward.

"Good morning," he said, "this is a splendid morning for a round. We don't start for half an hour yet. Allow me to introduce you to your partner," he went on, turning to a youngish-looking man standing beside him — "Mr. Nelson, Mr. Gibson."

We both bowed.

"I'm afraid you are getting rather a poor partner, Mr. Nelson; I haven't been playing for some time, except a round yesterday ('hope he won't ask when I last played before that,' I thought), and am rather out of form in consequence."

"Oh, Nelson will pull you through," put in White; "he's a very strong player, and it ought to make a match. Adams and I are only kind of fairish. By the by, have you seen the new putter?" he said, turning to Adams.

"No," replied Adams, "but I have heard plenty about it. Have you got one?"

"Yes," answered White, "here it is." And, crossing the room, he came back with a club in his hands.

I must describe this club if you will have patience, reader.

The head was an oblong block, with the shaft coming up from the neck as usual. There was nothing very particular about that, barring the shaft. The grip was all right, but below it was a spring, which joined it to the shaft. The slightest motion of your hands on the grip made the club oscillate backwards and forwards, like a pendulum, the grip, however, remaining steady in your hands. On the back of the grip were a row of figures, 1, 2, 3, 4, 5, 6, 8, 10, 12, 15, 20, 25, 30, 40, 50, with a hand which you could push along to indicate any of them. If you put it at 1, the club would only waggle with strength enough to send the ball one foot. Whatever figure you put it at, the club would only send the ball the corresponding number of feet. Of course, if the ground was extra heavy or on a slope you had to allow for that. The way in which you played the shot may be described thus: you put the hand at the figure corresponding to the distance you were from the hole (and, of course, one soon got pretty good at judging that), held the club *over* the ball, and with a slight motion of your hands set it in motion. When you had got the right line to the hole,

*The slightest motion of your hands on the grip made the club oscil-
late backwards and forwards, like a pendulum, the grip, however,
remaining steady in your hands.*

you just put it down behind the ball, and thereupon it would send it the prescribed number of feet. Success was then a simple matter of judging the right line; if you were on that, you would hole out, or at the very least lie dead. Such was the latest thing in put- ters. We each got one, determined to give it a trial. When I had finished examining the weapon, I went forward to the window to have a look at the home of my boyhood. Was this, indeed, Golfton? Or was Adams playing a joke at my expense? Yes, there were some of the old landmarks, and there were the four islands dotted along the shore, as I so well remember them. Yet, when I looked more closely at one, it seemed to be altered. The top was more even, and there appeared to be some sort of building on it. I afterwards discovered they had a sort of electric shoot as a means of crossing the water to this island. You sat in a flat-bottomed machine, shaped something like a boat, and were shot out of a steep slide across the strait on to the island, which was laid out in terraces cut out of the solid rock—an arrangement which must be rather a surprise, I should think, for the rabbits and Tommy Norries, the only inhabitants there were in my days. A similar means of communication was used on the island in order to shoot you back again. Of course if the sea was rough it couldn't be done; it seemed a very risky kind of game, anyway; I don't think I'd like it. There's no use running needless risk, you know; good men are scarce—at least I suppose they are now, they used to be a hundred years ago.

The green at Golfton was completely altered. We began to play at what was in my day the eighth hole. A plantation which used to run alongside of the sixth, seventh, and eighth holes had disappeared—in fact, the club-house in which I was standing seemed to occupy its former site.

The old part of the green—that is to say, the first seven holes we had formerly played over—was now used only by boys, who, I may mention, were under as strict supervision as the men, the records of all their scores being kept. They were not allowed on the long round till they were fifteen years of age, and not even then unless they could do their round in a certain number of strokes. I think it was an

average for a week that counted; but I forget what
the figures were.

It was now our turn to start, and, seeing my
companions hurrying out, I followed. We had each, of
course, to pay the customary five shillings; but as we
were playing a foursome we did not participate in the
prize money. Adams, I may mention, had sent my
clubs down below to be supplied with a caddie, who —
(if I must use the name) — but I can hardly call that
patent mechanical contrivance who. However, we
were all met by our several caddies.

"You will drive here," said Nelson, coming up to
me; "Adams will drive against you, and White and I
will drive together."

I selected my driver and proceeded to address
the ball. I felt in good form, and put my back into it.

"Fore!" Confound the thing! I had forgotten all
about that jacket. But it was a good drive, none the
less — it was perhaps just as well I *had* forgotten. If I
had been thinking about what was to come, I might
have — if I may be allowed to use slang — "funked" it. I
may mention that on looking at the dial on the sole of

the club, I found 195 yards was registered as the length of "carry"—so there evidently was something in their patents after all. Moreover the wind—at least all there was of it—was against us. Adams drove, and we all moved on. It was a funny sight to see four men stalking along followed by what looked like toy tricycles or something of that sort. The first hole was what was in my day the eleventh hole in; a steep bunker ran round two sides of it. White put his second in the bunker, while my partner carried everything and got on the green. Here the patent putter came into use. I put it at twenty-five feet, but it stopped about five feet short. Evidently I had been wrong in my calculation. However, my partner holed it, and we won the hole. The next was over a burn, which was carried in your second. We both managed it, and the hole was halved.

I now hardly noticed the jacket—so keen was I on the game, that I forgot all about it. Adams was right after all, therefore, in saying I would get used to it.

Going to the third hole, my partner put me in a bunker, in getting out of which I was nearly blinded with the revolving niblick. We also won that hole, and after we had played the first nine we were leading by five. I was playing quite a good game, better than even Adams or White—much to their disgust. At the ninth hole we came to a large pavilion, where Adams said we would stop for lunch. It occupied the same site as a cottage stood on in my days. It commanded a magnificent view. As you sat at lunch you saw spread out before you—not a table, of course, I'm not referring to the edibles—a long line of rocky shore with several islands dotted along it. The links we had been playing over stretched away from our very feet, and on the rising ground to the south of the course were numerous large villas scattered about, which were of course new to me. To the left of the first teeing ground—in what had formerly been a field where you lost two strokes if you drove into, not to mention the ball—stood a large hotel. The view from it must have been very fine, looking along what we used to call the "broad sands." That was a solitary place enough in my day, but now it seemed alive with bands, bathers, and children. Often on a quiet summer's evening I have watched the sun set behind the picturesque island of "Ardif." It was a view I remember well—and I don't suppose the sun sets anyway different in the twenty-first century!

But for the present I wasn't watching sunsets; I was at lunch—that's more to the point, eh? No, no, don't be frightened, I'm not going to give you another lecture on food. I'm going to practise now what I preached before, and, *entre nous,* dear reader, that's a thing I would like to see done more often by the genus preacher.

During the meal I noticed that both Adams and White were rather silent. I suspected that when they arranged the match they thought they would have somewhat the best of it. They did not count on me coming away with a good game. But Nelson and I were of course in great form, chaffing them about their game, and we finished up by offering them a stroke a hole going home—which they did not accept. After a good lunch and a smoke we started to play back. You see the course was so long now that one required a rest in the middle of it. The teeing ground at the ninth hole was in fact a second starting place. You just got your old place. Some couples went right round without stopping; but they were so few that it didn't matter, the other couples just falling in behind them. On the way home matters did not improve for Adams and his partner, and we ultimately won by six up and five to play, winning the bye also by two holes.

"Look here," said Adams, when we had finished, turning to me, "you're a fraud! You've no business to play a game like that after lying—Ahem! achew! ahem!" Here he took a fit of coughing to cover his mistake. He had nearly let out the secret.

"Yes," I said, "I seem to have got into my game all right again; but I don't think you were playing your game."

"Humph," he rejoined, "never had such hard lines in my life. If we'd had half the luck you had, the game would have ended very differently."

The same old excuses, I thought. Among all those inventions, surely they might have got something new in *that* line. However, I said nothing. It is no use trying to argue with a man in that frame of mind. You may mildly hint that bad luck generally goes with bad play; but it very seldom does any good. Your opponent will perhaps rejoin that it must be seldom indeed *you* win a match, you're swaggering so much about that one. The best thing is to leave him alone, stand him a whisky and soda, and light your pipe. Under this treatment he will gradually come round.

I know that kind of man well, and if he wants you to play to-morrow, why play him, and see that you give him another licking.

"What do you say to a shoot across to the 'Craig'?" said Nelson, my partner, as we were sitting in the club; "we have plenty of time."

"Capital," said White, "the very thing; I've been across several times, and the sensation is splendid. Come along."

"It doesn't look a very safe affair," I put in, mildly; "I think we would be better on dry land."

"Safe? It's as safe as going to church," said Nelson, "and it's a splendidly calm day. I've seen several boats shooting over."

"All right," I said, "I'm game; but at the same time, if there's an insurance office handy, I think we should each take out a policy."

We had to walk some little distance in an easterly direction, till we came to a high steel erection. Here we each put a shilling in that fail-me-never slot, and ascended in a lift. On leaving the lift we found ourselves on a narrow platform running round three sides of a small room. In the centre was the boat—for I suppose it was a boat—that was to convey us over the water. It was about twelve feet long by seven feet broad, rounded off at the corners, with the gunwale turned in all round, higher in front than at the back. It was seated for four, who were accommodated on seats all looking the same way—two in front and two behind—and set very low, not more than a few inches off the bottom. We took our seats, and Adams asked us if we were all ready. I gripped my seat tight. I did not like it at all. I sat looking down a long tube—it looked very steep, and the water very far away.

When we had all answered in the affirmative, Adams turned round to a man in a small box

In an instant we were on the water. As soon as we had touched the surface we bounded about five hundred yards, I should say. . . .

behind, whom I had not previously noticed, and said "right."

In an instant we were on the water. As soon as we had touched its surface we bounded about five hundred yards, I should say, and then about three hundred, getting shorter every time, just as a stone does when you skiff it along the surface of the water. On nearing the island the bounds got much shorter, and we ended by gliding into a small harbour, where we disembarked. The sensation on the whole was very pleasant, and the trip altogether did not last much more than a minute.

"Well, how did you like it?" asked Adams.

"I liked it very well," I answered, "though I must say at first I was rather frightened."

We strolled about the island for some time. It was not at all like the place that I remembered as the haunt of seabirds and rabbits. It was now all laid out in terraces cut out of the rock, with one or two places for refreshment. After we had seen all there was to be seen, we took our places for the return trip—I think I said before there was an erection on the island for shooting you back. The return journey was much the same as the first, and we arrived all safe, very pleased with the novel trip, as it was to me.

When Adams and I got home again we made our way to the morning-room, and there found Miss Adams busy writing. She was evidently deeply engrossed in her task, as she did not look up immediately.

"You are back before us to-day," said her brother, crossing the room.

"Yes," she answered, looking up, and laying down her pen, "I've been in some little time. Allow me to congratulate you on winning your match, Mr. Gibson."

"Thank you, Miss Adams," I said. "But how were you aware that I *did* win the match?"

"That's easily answered," she replied. "If I had not seen it by your face, I need only have looked at my brother's to see that he had lost."

"Do we indeed show it so plainly as that?" I said. "I had no idea that any one by merely looking at us could tell which had won the match."

"Undoubtedly you do," she went on. "When you lose a golf match you look as if you had lost a kingdom. Look at my brother there. Defeat is written on every line of his countenance. We women don't know what defeat means. When we lose what we are aiming at one time it only excites us to greater efforts the next. To be defeated is to be crushed, subdued. Did you ever see a subdued woman, even in your days?"

"Well—no—I—don't—think—I—ever—did," I had hesitatingly to admit, after consideration.

"And you have seen plenty of subdued men. If you lose a golf match you think life is not worth living; but fill you with meat and drink, and you are quite content. Ah! You men, you turn at every puff of wind. You are like the weathercocks, perched high on a pillar of your own conceit, imagining yourselves the lords of creation, yet obedient in turn to every breeze that blows. We women are made of different stuff."

"You're right," put in her brother; "it would never do to go by a female weathercock—weatherhen I suppose I should call it. If the wind were east, it would point due west; and if south, it would point due

north, out of sheer contradictoriness. I expect that
was kept in mind when people chose the male bird."

"You do not understand the sex," she said; "in
fact, you do not even understand your own sex. But I
am glad we occupy our right position in the world at
last. I sometimes pity the women of bygone ages.
What poor, weak creatures they were!"

"Allow me to differ from you," I put in. "If you
will pardon the seeming rudeness, I think they were
superior in every way to the women of to-day, to judge
from what I have seen."

(That's a slap on the face for her, I thought.) But
she only smiled.

"Quite right to stick up for your own age," she
said; "but that does not alter facts."

I made some excuse, and left the room. I really
couldn't bear it; and if I had stayed there much longer
we should have come to blows, I know. Poor Adams! I
feel sorry for him. No wonder he looks subdued
sometimes.

And I had had a day at Golfton! Golfton in the
year 2000! How different it was from the Golfton of

1892! The same; yet not the same. Many a match I've won—aye, faith, and lost too, too many of them—on that old green, without the aid of patent caddies, self-registering clubs, and shouting "fore" jackets. Those good old days! They seem to have nothing in common with this age of new inventions. I think I like the old days best after all. And yet I don't know, they manage everything so well now, that I think I should get on all right if I just *steer clear of the ladies.*

CHAPTER X.

GOLF-WARS — WE SEE THE AMERICAN MATCH IN LONDON —
DORNOCH WINS — THE DINNER — ADAMS'S SPEECH —
I MAKE MYSELF KNOWN — FINIS.

A week had now passed, and the close of it found me still the guest of Mr. Adams, and enjoying myself, to use slang, "down to the ground." I had quite got into my golf, and was playing a first-rate game. I had visited several greens, including some that I had played on before (a hundred years before, I mean) and others that were quite new to me, and had found each one more charming than the last. In fact, I could not

137

make up my mind which one I would settle down to play permanently on. Of course everybody stuck to his own green; if you visited others you did not participate in the daily prize-money, unless on special days. I thought I would look well about me before finally settling.

Golf, I think I told you before, was the business of the male population, while the women, the females—females is the best word to express the gentler sex now, though I don't think they would like to hear me calling them the gentler sex, and, in fact, I don't think they are, but they won't see this book, so it does not matter; and the 1892 ladies, bless their little hearts!—but I'm not going to say anything about them; words fail me . . . Well, those double-distilled females of 2000 looked after all these trivial matters, such as Church and State, financial establishments, and so on. Why, we men really hadn't time for things of that kind. The invention of a new putter was of more importance than a European war; though I should mention, by the way, that wars had ceased in Europe. They had come to be too much of a farce.

Guns, rifles, &c., were out of date altogether. They had invented some kind of gas which, encased in a bomb, could be projected any distance up to one hundred miles, and then made to burst. When it burst it turned everybody within a radius of ten miles insensible, and they remained so for about two days. Thus one shot would render a whole army *hors de combat*. An agreement was therefore come to among the powers of Europe that wars should cease, and disputes should instead be settled by—by what do you think? Why, *golf matches*. There is a triumph for golf! Fancy the fate of an empire hanging on a putt—the hopes of a country shattered by a bad lying ball! What do you think of that, you 1892 golfers, who look glum when you have to hand over your half-crowns? There, surely, was something to incite the youthful golfer. His was the prospect of perhaps representing his country on the field of battle, or what now was the field of battle. What patriotic feelings must stir your manly bosom when you grasped your driver, or seized your niblick with a do-or-die look about you! Why, Horatius and all those old fogies wouldn't be in it with you.

These matches were, however, very rare. They were played by a hundred men a-side—fifty playing in the one country and fifty in the other, and each couple on a separate green. You may judge of the excitement such matches caused in the country—or the world, for the matter of that. They were watched eagerly by crowds in every large town, and the position of the whole match was known at every hole. If a Frenchman missed a short putt at Pau, it was seen, and chuckled over, through the whole of Great Britain.

The match which I referred to before, between Jack Dornoch—or, to give him his correct title, Sir John Dornoch—and the American, Michigan, was coming off; so Adams and I went up to London to see it. It could be watched in our own town, but Adams had some business—golfing business, of course—in London on that day, and we thought we would kill two birds with one stone.

After he had finished his business we made our way to a large hall in Oxford Street, put a shilling in the slot, and went in. It was an immense hall with three tiers of galleries, seated for about five or six thousand people. We got good seats, well forward, in a part railed off for golf officials. The rest of the hall was packed. The glass on which we were to see the match represented was at first dark; but on a bell sounding it got suddenly bright, while the rest of the hall was darkened. Represented on the glass were a number of men standing about, all life-size. The match was evidently just going to begin. It was actually being played in America, you must remember, at that moment, though not, of course, at the same hour of the day. By the by, we rather score off the go-ahead Yankees there. They fancy they can keep ahead of us, but in the matter of time we're always a little in front. Suddenly everybody moved aside, and a tall young fellow stepped forward. This, my companion informed me, was Dornoch. He drove off, and was followed by his adversary, Michigan, who was a shorter though stouter-built man. When they had both driven they walked on. The effect was very curious. You saw them walking, yet they never moved from the same

It was an immense hall with three tiers of galleries, seated for about five or six thousand people.

part of the glass. The ground glided behind them, but as the hall was darkened and the glass was the only part of the hall lighted up, you did not notice that. They looked quite natural walking along. The American had to play the odds. The ball, after it was struck, vanished. Of course you could not follow its flight, as the glass only took in a few yards round the players. They both reached the green in three. The putting was much the most interesting part of the game to watch, as you saw the ball from start to finish. The first hole was halved in five, as also the second. The third Dornoch managed to secure by a long putt, and led by one, but this temporary advantage he did not maintain, as the American squared matters at the next hole, and, moreover, improved his position by winning the next two. It was now the Scotchman's turn, and he took full advantage of it by winning two out of the next three holes. Thus the match stood all square at the turn. The first hole in fell to Dornoch, his opponent being bunkered off his second, and the next three being halved, matters were looking slightly

healthy for the Scotchman, especially after the next.
hole, which he won, thus standing two up with four
to play. He lost the next, however, and the sixteenth
being halved, he now stood one up with two to play.

The excitement in the hall was tremendous,
every shot being watched with deep interest, and
shouts of, "Hurry up, Yankee Doodle!" and "Well
played, Sir John!" broke in every now and again. That
was one advantage in watching a match that was
being played four thousand miles away. You could
make as much row as you liked, it did not disturb the
players. I must say, however, the audience, under the
circumstances, kept remarkably quiet, only some
exceptionable bits of play being greeted by shouts of
approval. The second last hole was a great one for the
Scotchman. He was lying badly in a bunker, just off
the putting green, while Michigan was within two
yards of the hole. They had both played four, and
Dornoch was giving the odds. He took his niblick and
put his back into it. It looked as if he had emptied
the bunker, and for a second he could not be seen for
the sand. I was watching him, when a deafening

shout almost lifted the roof off the building. He had holed it. The ball had not landed on the green and rolled into the hole; it had lofted right in and stayed there—a fluke, of course, but a wonderful shot. Michigan had only this for a half, and he studied his putt with great care. The first half of a hole is proverbially the best.

He addressed himself to the ball, and played it. It stopped just on the lip of the hole. First a deep sigh, and then a shout went up from every throat in the hall. Dornoch had won the match by two up and one to play. It was an exciting enough finish in all conscience. They did not play the last hole, but walked in, and we lost sight of them, the glass again being darkened and the hall lit up. It was wonderful. No anxious waiting for the next morning's papers to see the result of a match now. Here was I, four thousand miles away from the scene of action, watching every shot played as if I had been on the green itself.

Adams was in great form at the result of the match, having won his money. He had been backing Dornoch to some extent.

"That's something of a novelty for you," he said
to me, as we were leaving.

"True," I answered, "but I am getting used to all
that kind of thing now."

"Oh, by the by," he went on, "White and Nelson,
and one or two others, are going to dine with me to-
night. I've never introduced you properly to my
friends; but I will to-night, though of course there's
no need to tell them everything. They'll all be very
pleased at the result of the match, and so they ought
to be — it's quite a national victory. You see we can still
hold our own as golfers, as well as everything else,
though, for the latter, we leave that, as you know, to
the women, and as long as they've got anything to do
with it there's no fear of Britain being anywhere but
in the front rank."

So Adams ran on as we made our way home.
He was evidently in great spirits over the match,
and he never stopped talking till we got into the
house. He spoke of nothing but golf and golfers —
golfers who had died, and golfers still living — and
we got into quite a hot discussion as to whether

Allan Robertson and some other nineteenth-century players whom he named — he called them the fathers of golf — played as good a game in their day as was played now, of course allowing for the rude, old-fashioned clubs they used. (Talking about rude, old-fashioned clubs, I remember some very rude, old-fashioned players, but that is "buy the whey," as the milkman said.) I maintained that they did. He said they didn't, and we were still fighting it out when we found ourselves once more under his friendly roof.

I hurried off to prepare myself for dinner, and when I was ready I went to the pink room, where I found Adams ready waiting for his guests.

I don't think I told you before that gentlemen's evening dress had undergone a marked improvement. Only in it did they allow themselves to appear in any kind of colour. Through the day their dress was of the most sombre description.

I must say I was glad when I saw they had done away with those black coats and white shirt-fronts, in which you could never tell a gentleman from a waiter unless he had an eyeglass—the gentlemen, of course. I never did see a waiter with an eyeglass. The dress now consisted of a scarlet jacket, a white silk waistcoat, and scarlet silk knee-breeches, with white silk stockings and scarlet shoes. Very pretty it was.

The company soon began to arrive, and when they had all assembled, to the number of about twenty, we made our way down—dash it all, I very nearly said downstairs again! Most of them I had met before. They were all golfers, I need not say, in an age when everybody played. Miss Adams, I am glad to say, was not at dinner. She was engaged in London on parliamentary business or something of that sort. It was just as well. Had she been there she would have acted like the proverbial wet blanket. She wasn't a kindred spirit. We had a first-rate dinner, with plenty of fizz. Everybody was in great form, and jokes and golfing anecdotes were flying about like squibs on the 5th of November. I wish I could remember some of them. One I do recall, though, and I'll tell it to you. It was Adams's anecdote, and was about a nineteenth-century golfer, which gave

my host occasion to look at me as he told it. A golf
club committee were revising the handicaps the
night before a match. It was proposed to raise one
old fellow's handicap, when a member interposed.
"Jist leave it alane," he said, *he's a gay guid coonter.*"
There were many more, but I do not remember
them. One story at a time, as the man said when he
fell over the window.

It was getting pretty late, when old Fitzroy, a
guest with a very red face, who was sitting next
Adams, and had been concealing a good quantity of
champagne about his person during the evening,
rose, put both hands in his pockets, looked round the
table, and smiled across to me.

"Shentlemen," he said, "I'm going to give you a
tosht, drink a hel—hic—hish. I'm not customed—
hic—to undress meetingsh." Here we all burst out
laughing; he looked rather annoyed, but went on: "but
I shink on—hic—thish suspicious—hic—occasion—"
Here we all simply roared, and kept on laughing for
about five minutes, when he sat down muttering,
"Don't know what—hic—got to laugh at."

*"Shentlemen," he said, "I'm going to give you a tosht, drink a hel—
hic—hish. I'm not customed—hick—to undress meetingsh."*

He sat very quiet and glum after that; I was rather sorry for the old chap.

Adams now got up.

"Gentlemen," he said, "Mr. Fitzroy was about to propose the health of my friend Mr. Gibson, and though the spirit was willing enough, the flesh was weak. I'm afraid I'll not be able to do it as well as he would. I shall content myself with few words. I want you all to extend to Mr. Gibson the hand of friendship, the golfer's hand of friendship. He is a true golfer in this age when every man is a golfer and every golfer a true golfer. Gentlemen, here's long life to Mr. Gibson, and may his golf always improve."

The toast was drunk with great enthusiasm. I, of course, had to reply—I'm awfully bad at making speeches, but I couldn't get out of it, so I thought I would just tell them who I was, about lying for so long and all that.

"Gentlemen," I began, "thank you all very much for the cordial way in which you drank my health. As Mr. Adams said, I am a golfer, I hope a true one, and strange as it may sound, I began golf before any one in this room was born. In fact I first played golf in the year 1876. No, I'm not drunk, but I thought that would surprise you. I think most of you know of that living corpse, if I may call it so, that Adams has had for years lying in his house. Not only the skeleton, but the whole body, in the cupboard. Well, gentlemen, I am that body come to life again."

They were all gazing at me in wonder. Most of them had seen me as the corpse, but of course they could not recognise me without the beard, &c.

"Yes, gentlemen, for one hundred and eight years, as Adams will tell you, I lay in a trance. In my former existence I was a golfer, in my present existence I am a golfer, and in my future existence I hope still to be a golfer" (this statement was greeted with great applause), "though how they will play golf in that future existence I am frightened to think. You seem to have brought it as near perfection as it is possible. This was the dream of my nineteenth-century life—a dream that I little thought would be realised. And now, gentlemen, I must again thank you for the kindly welcome you have given me, and I hope that we will all have many a tough fight yet on the links."

When I sat down they all crowded round me, and I had to answer dozens of questions. It was evidently to be a secret no longer, so I determined to see the doctors on the morrow, and get my money, &c.

At last everybody had gone, and I made my way up to my room.

Now, dear reader, this tale is ended. But don't think I'm going to bed to wake up in the morning, and find myself back in 1892 again, and this all a dream. No, no; I'm in 2000, and in 2000 I mean to stay. It suits me far better than ever 1892 did with all its work and its worry. The year 2000 is the year for me, and if I meet any of your great-great-great-grand-children going about, I'll put them up to a wrinkle or two. So, gentle reader, for the present "good-bye," and if I come across anything more that I think will interest you I'll let you know. So ta, ta.

FINIS.

AFTERWORD

It's hard to believe this book was written in 1892. The author's nineteenth-century preview of the future is uncanny, even if the book's specific details of technological and societal changes sometimes fail to match present-day reality.

In full appreciation of the visionary talents of the author, J. McCullough, also known as J.A.C.K., the following brief inventory of some of the prophetic "highlights" of *Golf in the Year 2000* also notes the years in which McCullough's fictional creations became commonplace:

- Chapter 2 mentions "an ordinary sized signet ring with the figures 6.34 on it" similar to digital (albeit wrist) watches that came into vogue soon after the introduction of quartz crystal watches, circa 1970 – about **eighty years** after the publication of *Golf in the Year 2000.*

- In chapter 3, the author portrays a world in which color photography has replaced color paintings as the preferred choice of portrait artists. In 1907 – **fifteen years** after the book's publication – Autochrome photo plates were introduced, moving natural-color photography beyond the experimental stage.

- The supersonic underground tubular railways first mentioned in chapter 4 involved technology far beyond anything seen in 1892. In 1964 – **seventy-two years later** – Japan's *Shinkansen,* the world's first "bullet train," entered service. It was soon achieving speeds

in excess of 150 miles per hour. Even now, the
world is still trying to catch up to
McCullough: His subterranean passenger
train was not only intercontinental, it was
able to cover the London-to-New York route
in about two and a half hours, averaging more
than one thousand miles per hour!

- Chapter 5 describes our story's protagonist,
  Alexander Gibson, getting his first taste of the
  automated golf caddie, a mechanical club-car-
  rying contraption that follows the golfer
  around the course thanks to a homing device
  attached to the back of the golfer's belt. Such
  a device first appeared on real golf courses in
  the early 1980s—about **ninety years** after
  McCullough wrote the book.

- Also in chapter 5, Gibson gets his first crack
  at metal woods—the shafts are made of steel
  (instead of hickory) and the clubheads are
  metal (in place of persimmon). Metal

clubheads were experimental at the time the book was written; however, the first patent for steel shafts was issued to Arthur Knight of Schenectady, New York, in 1910 — **eighteen years** later. Metal woods with steel or other metal-alloy shafts have become popular among the masses in the 1990s — about **one hundred years** after *Golf in the Year 2000*.

- A form of televised golf is explained in chapter 6 as the transmission of images through a networked system of mirrors. Granted, no sound is able to accompany these images being viewed by theater patrons hundreds of miles away, but the idea of lining golf courses with mirrors atop poles indicates an intense societal interest in "televised" golf. Some purists would say that golf emerged as a televised sport in the late 1950s with the emergence of Arnold Palmer, but the first official golf telecast was in 1938 by the BBC — even then, a full **forty-six years** after the book was written.

- Also in chapter 6, J.A.C.K. introduces the
International Championship, an annual event
pitting two teams of twenty golfers against
each other. Further mention of a similar international competition involving the United
States suddenly sounds very much like the
biennial Ryder Cup competitions, which have
emerged as golf's version of the Olympics.
The first Ryder Cup Match was in 1927 —
thirty-five years later.

- The main character, Gibson, unwittingly
gets a glimpse of feminism late in chapter 6
when he muses that he did not notice any
women on the streets — only men. But in
chapter 7, Adams tells Gibson that women
wear the same attire as men, which makes it
nearly impossible to distinguish men from
women at a distance. Gibson further discov-
ers just how far women have come when he
meets Adams's sister, who, like most women
of the era, is a business executive: Women

run the business world, while men mostly
play golf. While women's suffrage in the
early twentieth century gave American
women the right to vote, the seeds of feminism were not planted until much later. One
landmark to the feminist movement was the
1964 publication of Betty Friedan's
The Feminist Mystique — **seventy-two years**
after *Golf in the Year 2000!*

A number of other predictions merit special
attention, among them automatic interior lighting
tied to the movement of the sun, golf balls with a core
of compressed air, the infamous "fore" jacket, chemi-
cals to induce and stop rainfall, spring-loaded pendulum putters, speedboats, and long-range missiles.
Some of these have become reality in one form or
another, while others perhaps remain on someone's
drawing board.